KB244461

Gold Rush!

About Wise & Wide

- A systematic 6-level English reading program based on Lexile® measures
- Diverse and interesting topics chosen from the elementary curriculums of Korea and English speaking western countries
- Well-written books in various forms including fiction stories, descriptive texts, and classics retold
- The informative but original fiction stories grab your interest, leading to the easy and clear understanding of the educational content.
- Improve thinking skills with solid after-reading activities at all levels of the series.

Wise & Wide is a 6-level English reading program that consists of 60 books and each level is systematically divided by Lexile® measures. The Lexile® Framework for Reading is the most popular reading measuring system in American formal education curriculums and many English programs. Over 20 out of 50 states in the U.S. mark Lexile® measures directly on students' final report cards and over 300 well-known publishers adopt and use Lexile® measures.

Experience many kinds of readings written by professional writers from the U.S. and England. They used interesting topics that were carefully chosen after analyzing elementary curriculums from around the world including Korea, the U.S., England, and Australia among many others. Comprehensive after-reading activities including graphic organizers, speaking tasks, and After-reading Tests are ready for you.

Levels in the series and their corresponding Lexile® measures

Level	Lexile® measures	U.S. Grade
Level 1	Below 200L	Pre K - K
Level 2	190L - 400L	Lower Grade 1
Level 3	350L - 530L	Upper Grade 1
Level 4	420L - 650L	Grade 2
Level 5	520L - 940L	Grade 3 - 4
Level 6	830L - 1070L	Grade 5 - 6

＊ Smart Readers: Wise & Wide level 1 is applicable to the preschool level in the U.S.

＊ The source of the relationship between Lexile® measures and U.S. school grades: CCSS(Common Core State Standards) FOR ENGLISH LANGUAGE ARTS, APPENDIX A (2012, which is used by 45 states in the U.S.)

Topic List

	Level 1	Level 2	Level 3	Level 4	Level 5	Level 6
Book 1	Science>Biology: The hibernation of animals Story	Science>Biology: Living and nonliving things Story	Science>Biology> Animals & the Environment: Sea otters Story	Environment> Living with nature: The diver & the persimmon tree Story	Science>Biology> Animal: Amazing animals of the Amazon Story	Science>Biology: Germs, transmitted diseases Story
Book 2	Literature> World classics: Aesop's fables Story	Literature> Traditional fairy tale: Old tales about stones Story	Social Studies> Economy: To run a business to make and save money Story	Science>Biology> Plants: Photosynthesis Story	Science>Earth science: Earth's layers, earthquakes, volcanoes, and earth's atmosphere Report	Mathematics> Sequence: The golden ratio & the Fibonacci sequence Story
Book 3	Science>Physics: How shadows are formed Story	Literature> World classics: Peter Pan Story	Science>Scientific technology: Nanobots Story	Literature>Myths: World's creation stories Story	Literature> Legend: The story of King Arthur Story	Literature>Myths: Constellation myths Story
Book 4	Literature> Traditional literature: The Talmud Story	Science>Biology> Animal: Polar bears Story	Science>Biology> Animal: Mountain gorillas Story	Social Studies> Cultural anthropology: Amazing ancient cultures of the world Story	Science> Earth science: Clouds and weather Story	Literature> Human & animals: The friendship between a girl and a horse Story
Book 5	Social Studies> Ethics: Rules in daily life Story	Science>Biology: The five senses Report	Social Studies> Cultural anthropology: Astonishing festivals Report	Art>Music: Stories from two operas Story	Social Studies> World culture & history: The Renaissance Story	Sports> Board sports: Surfing & snowboarding Story
Book 6	Social Studies> World geography & travel: Tourist attractions around the world Story	Science>Biology> Animal: Dinosaurs Story	Science> Astronomy: The solar system Story	Social Studies> People: Three great people who overcame hardships Story	Science>Scientific technology: The wonderful world of robots Report	Art>Music: Composers of the Romantic Era Report
Book 7	Science> Space science: The life of astronauts Report	Social Studies> Cultural anthropology: Mythological monsters from around the world Report	Mathematics> Elementary mathematics: Numbers, measurement, shapes and data Report	Science & Social Studies> Technology & culture: Inventions from around the world Report	Art>Works of art: Famous paintings Report	Social Studies> Human & animals: Animals in action for human Report
Book 8	Social Studies> Cultural anthropology: Various living cultures of the world Story	Art>Music: Instruments in the orchestra Story	Social Studies> Life safety: Learning and using outdoor survival skills Story	Social Studies> History: The California Gold Rush Report	Social Studies & Science> Psychology: Psychology in everyday life Story	Literature> World classics: The Merchant of Venice Story
Book 9	Social Studies> Jobs: Interviews about jobs Report	Science>Scientific technology: Developments in technology in different times Story	Social Studies> Politics>Election: Running for 3rd grade class president Story	Literature> World classics: Stories of Sherlock Holmes Story	Literature> World classics: Adrift in the Pacific Story	
Book 10		Sports>Winter sports: Various aspects of some Winter Olympic sports Report				

* 10 books in each level will be published.

How to Use This Book

• Before Reading

You can easily find the topic and what kind of story you are about to read.

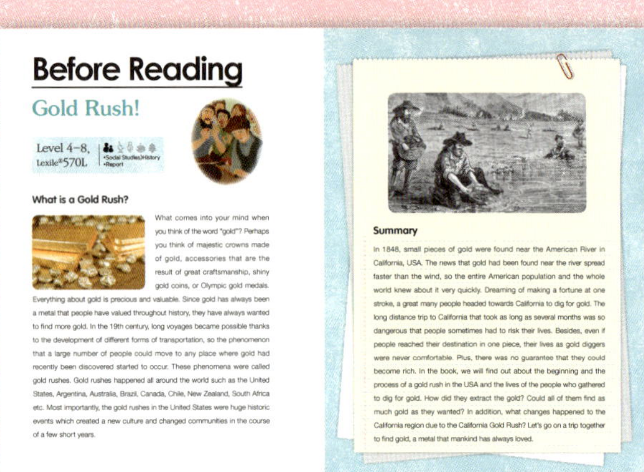

• The text

All the stories were written by professional writers from the U.S. and England, so you will read authentic and appropriate English sentences and expressions in every book in the series.

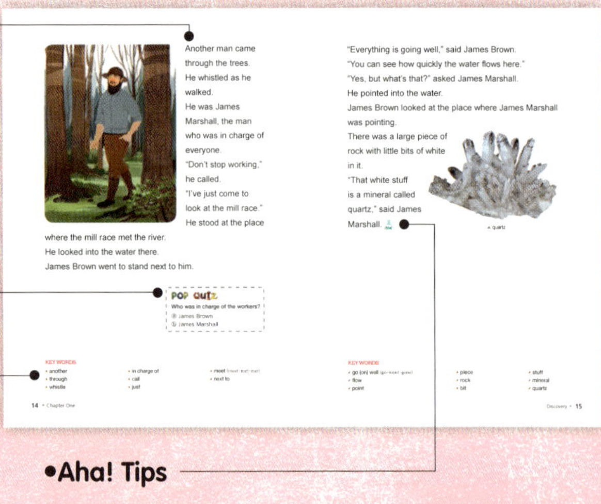

• Pop Quiz

Check out right away if you understand what you have just read by solving a pop quiz that checks your comprehension.

• Key Words

The key words and expressions on each page are listed for you to easily study them.

• Aha! Tips

Download free Korean explanations at *www.ihappyhouse.co.kr* for all of the sentences marked with "Aha!". These explain cultural, scientific, and economic knowledge or they deal with aspects of English such as grammatical structures or idiomatic expressions. There are lots of "Aha! Tips" to help you understand the text.

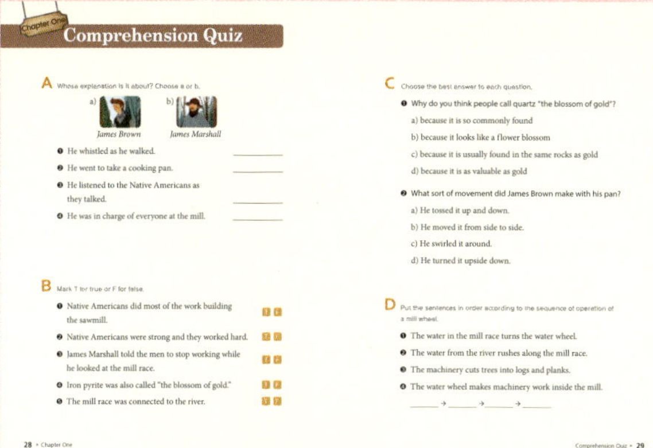

•Comprehension Quiz

After reading one chapter, solve various questions to find out if you fully understand the content.

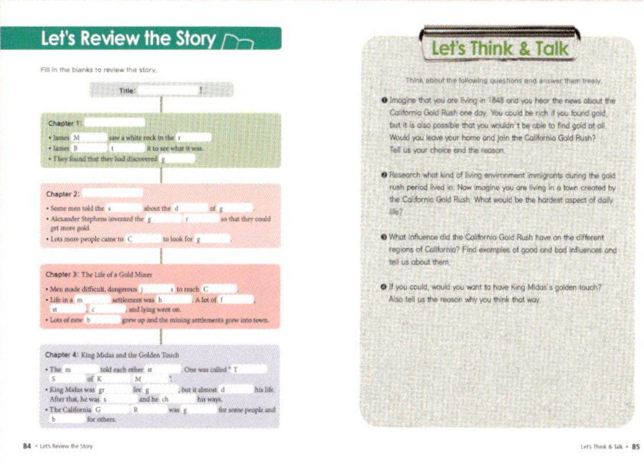

•Let's Review the Story / •Let's Think & Talk

Fill in the blanks in the organizer to summarize the whole story. Express your own thinking and feelings about the story by answering the questions. You can build up logic and reasoning skills for your essay examinations in the future.

Appendix

Audio CD

In the CD audio book form, the texts are read vividly by American professional voice actors. (MP3 files downloaded for free)

After-reading Test

Solve an additionally provided After-reading Test for each book.

The Korean translation, Answer Keys, a Word Quiz, a Word List, and Aha! Tips for each book

You can download them for free at *www.ihappyhouse.co.kr* or *www.darakwon.co.kr*

Before Reading

Gold Rush!

Level 4–8,
Lexile®570L | •Social Studies〉History
•Report

What is a Gold Rush?

What comes into your mind when you think of the word "gold"? Perhaps you think of majestic crowns made of gold, accessories that are the result of great craftsmanship, shiny gold coins, or Olympic gold medals. Everything about gold is precious and valuable. Since gold has always been a metal that people have valued throughout history, they have always wanted to find more gold. In the 19th century, long voyages became possible thanks to the development of different forms of transportation, so the phenomenon that a large number of people could move to any place where gold had recently been discovered started to occur. These phenomena were called gold rushes. Gold rushes happened all around the world such as the United States, Argentina, Australia, Brazil, Canada, Chile, New Zealand, South Africa etc. Most importantly, the gold rushes in the United States were huge historic events which created a new culture and changed communities in the course of a few short years.

Summary

In 1848, small pieces of gold were found near the American River in California, USA. The news that gold had been found near the river spread faster than the wind, so the entire American population and the whole world knew about it very quickly. Dreaming of making a fortune at one stroke, a great many people headed towards California to dig for gold. The long distance trip to California that took as long as several months was so dangerous that people sometimes had to risk their lives. Besides, even if people reached their destination in one piece, their lives as gold diggers were never comfortable. Plus, there was no guarantee that they could become rich. In the book, we will find out about the beginning and the process of a gold rush in the USA and the lives of the people who gathered to dig for gold. How did they extract the gold? Could all of them find as much gold as they wanted? In addition, what changes happened to the California region due to the California Gold Rush? Let's go on a trip together to find gold, a metal that mankind has always loved.

Contents

Gold Rush!

Gold Rush!

Chapter One

Discovery

January 24, 1848

James Brown stood in the forest and looked up into the trees. Birds were singing there. They reminded him that spring was coming soon.

He could hear the rushing sound of the river nearby.

James Brown worked for John Sutter, who owned some land near the American River.

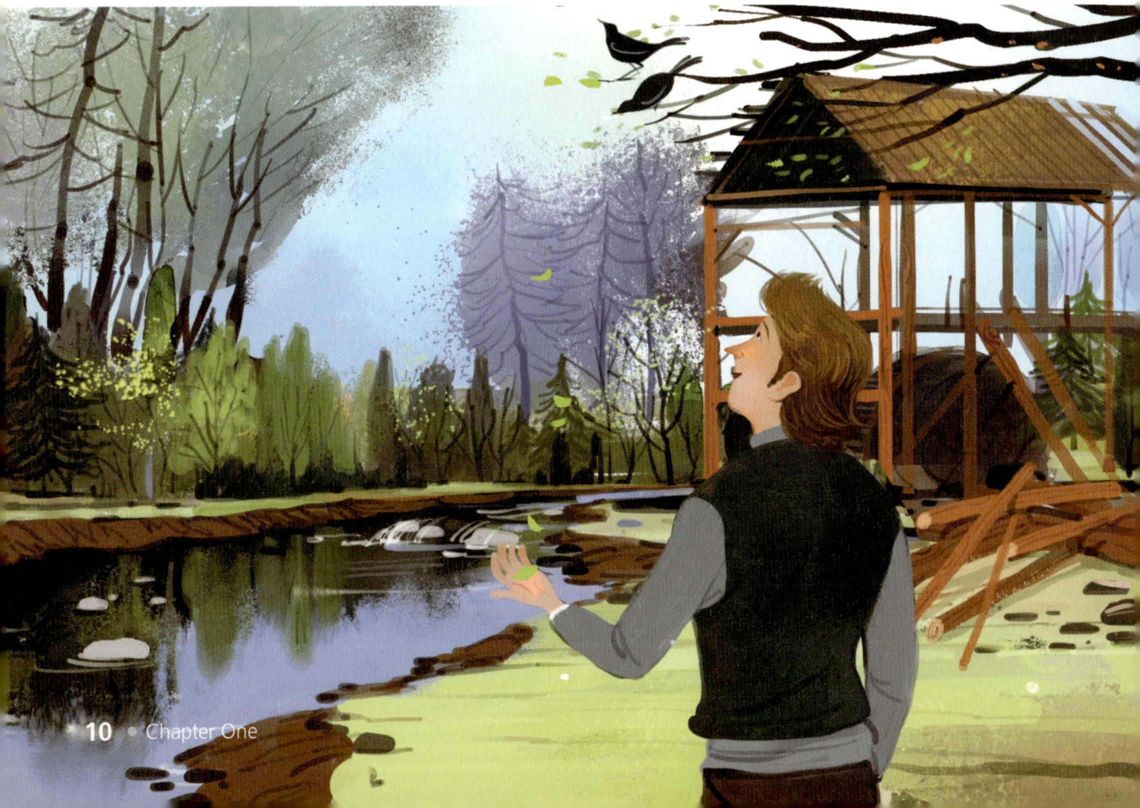

John Sutter was building a sawmill, a place where trees are cut into logs and planks.

There is a lot of work to do in building a mill so a lot of men worked for John Sutter.

Most of the hard work was done by the Native Americans. They had lived there for a long time.

They were strong and hard-working, even though they weren't paid very much.

James Brown spoke their language, so it was his job to tell them what to do.

KEY WORDS

- **stand** (stand-stood-stood)
- **forest**
- **look up**
- **remind**
- **spring**
- **soon**
- **rush**
- **sound**
- **nearby**
- **work**
- **own**
- **near**
- **build** (build-built-built)
- **sawmill**
- **log**
- **plank**
- **a lot of**
- **mill**
- **most**
- **hard**
- **Native American**
- **for a long time**
- **hard-working**
- **even though**
- **pay** (pay-paid-paid)
- **language**
- **job**

Now, he listened to them talking as they worked.

They knew this forest better than anyone.

James Brown stood back to let them get on with their work.

A group of white men stood near the river. They were digging a mill race.

James looked at the mill race. It was a narrow channel in the ground.

Water from the river rushed along it very quickly.

When the mill was finished, the rushing water would turn a huge wooden mill wheel.

In turn, the mill wheel would make machinery work inside the mill. *Aha!*

KEY WORDS

- **get on with** (get-got-gotten)
- **a group of**
- **white**
- **dig** (dig-dug-dug)(*cf.* dig up)
- **mill race**
- **narrow**
- channel
- ground
- along
- quickly
- finish
- turn
- huge
- wooden
- mill wheel
- in turn
- machinery
- inside

Another man came through the trees.
He whistled as he walked.
He was James Marshall, the man who was in charge of everyone.
"Don't stop working," he called.
"I've just come to look at the mill race."
He stood at the place where the mill race met the river.
He looked into the water there.
James Brown went to stand next to him.

KEY WORDS

- another
- through
- whistle
- in charge of
- call
- just
- meet (meet-met-met)
- next to

"Everything is going well," said James Brown.

"You can see how quickly the water flows here."

"Yes, but what's that?" asked James Marshall.

He pointed into the water.

James Brown looked at the place where James Marshall
was pointing.

There was a large piece of
rock with little bits of white
in it.

"That white stuff
is a mineral called
quartz," said James
Marshall.

▲ quartz

KEY WORDS

- **go (on) well** (go-went-gone)
- **flow**
- **point**
- piece
- rock
- bit
- stuff
- mineral
- quartz

"I don't think it is," said James Brown.

"It's just a common rock that you can find all over these hills."

"I'm sure it's quartz," said James Marshall.

He knelt by the river to look at the rock more closely.

"Do you know what people say when there is quartz in a rock?"

He looked up, his eyes gleaming with excitement. "They call it 'the blossom of gold'!"

Gold?  James Brown felt his heart beat more quickly. "Do you really think so?" he said.

He spoke quietly so that the other men wouldn't hear. He didn't want them to stop doing their work.

▲ quartz containing gold

KEY WORDS

- common
- all over
- hill
- sure
- kneel (kneel-knelt-knelt)
- closely
- gleam
- excitement
- blossom
- gold
- feel (feel-felt-felt)
- heart
- beat (beat-beat-beaten)
- quietly
- other

James Marshall nodded.

"I'm sure of it."

"Well, there's only one way to find out," said James Brown. "Wait here. I'll be back in a few minutes."

James Brown set off through the trees. At first, he walked. But soon he broke into a run.

Could it really be true that there was gold here?

KEY WORDS

- nod
- only
- **find out** (find-found-found)
- wait
- in a few minutes
- **set off** (set-set-set)
- at first

- break into a run
  (break-broke-broken)
- true
- hurry
- cabin
- shallow
- pan

- cook
- meat
- then
- still
- stare at

He hurried to his cabin and found a shallow pan that he
used for cooking meat.
Then, he rushed back to the mill race with the pan.
There he found James Marshall still staring at the rock with
many little bits of white in it.

James Brown dipped the pan into the water near the white rock. He scooped up some water, sand, and gravel from the bottom of the river.

He knew that gold was quite heavy. Any tiny pieces would fall to the bottom of the pan.

He swirled the pan around, hoping to see the gleam of gold. But there was nothing.

KEY WORDS

- dip
- scoop up
- gravel
- bottom

- quite
- heavy
- tiny
- **fall** (fall-fell-fallen)

- swirl
- around
- hope

▲ the place where James Marshall found gold
(By Bobak Ha'Eri (Own work) [CC BY 3.0
(http://creativecommons.org/licenses/by/3.0)], via Wikimedia Commons)

James Brown sighed, put the pan down, and stood up.

"There's nothing here after all," he said. His voice was filled with disappointment.

"I disagree," said James Marshall.

"Stay here and keep the men working. I will go and look further down the river."

He picked up the pan and hurried away, looking into the water the whole time.

"You won't find anything," James Brown called after him.

But James Marshall seemed not to hear.

James Brown shook his head and went to make sure the men were all working hard. Aha!

A little while later, James Marshall returned.

He was carrying the pan in one hand and something else in the other hand.

It looked like the woolen hat he had been wearing earlier.

He wore it to keep his head warm on cold mornings.

He could hardly speak for excitement.

"Brown!" he hissed.

"Come and see what I've found!"

KEY WORDS

- call after
- seem
- **shake one's head** (shake-shook-shaken)
- **make sure** (make-made-made)
- while
- later
- return
- carry

- else
- look like
- woolen
- **wear** (wear-wore-worn)
- earlier
- warm
- hardly
- hiss

He held out his hat for James Brown to see.

Lying in the bottom of the hat were around twelve small

flakes of something that looked like gold!

The two men called James stared at each other.

Smiles crept over their faces.

- **hold out** (hold-held-held)
- **lie** (lie-lay-lain)
- **flake**

- **each other**
- **creep over** (creep-crept-crept)
- **face**

But even though James Brown was smiling, he still couldn't believe it. With trembling fingers, he lifted one of the golden flakes and bit into it. It was hard between his teeth, but they left marks on it. That was a sure sign of gold. "We must test it some more to see if it really *is* gold," he said. "I know just how to do it."

POP QUIZ

How did James Brown test the golden flakes at first?

ⓐ He bit into one of them.
ⓑ He ate one of them.

KEY WORDS

- believe
- tremble
- lift
- golden
- bite (bite-bit-bitten)

- between
- teeth
- leave (leave-left-left)
- mark
- sure sign of

- must (= have to)
- test
- if
- how to + *Verb*

By this time, the other men had gathered to see what was going on.

They followed James Brown as he took the flake to his workbench and picked up a hammer.

He knew that there was another mineral that looked just like gold.

It was called iron pyrite. Aha!

But its other name was fool's gold.

It was important to make sure that this gold was not fool's gold.

▲ iron pyrite

KEY WORDS

- by this time
- gather
- go on
- follow

- **take** (take-took-taken)
- workbench
- hammer
- iron pyrite

- fool
- important

James Brown knew that real gold was soft.

It would not break into pieces when hit with a hammer. 

Fool's gold would shatter into lots of pieces.

The men held their breath.

James Brown hit the gold flake with the hammer.

It didn't shatter.

He turned to the waiting crowd and shouted, "Gold, boys, it really *is* gold!"

Which one would break into pieces when hit with a hammer?

ⓐ gold
ⓑ fool's gold

KEY WORDS

- real
- soft (↔ hard)
- break into pieces
- hit (hit-hit-hit)

- shatter
- hold one's breath
- crowd (*cf.* crowded)
- shout

Comprehension Quiz

A Whose explanation is it about? Choose a or b.

a) 

b) 

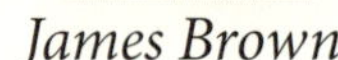

James Brown   *James Marshall*

❶ He whistled as he walked. _______________

❷ He went to take a cooking pan. _______________

❸ He listened to the Native Americans as
they talked. _______________

❹ He was in charge of everyone at the mill. _______________

B Mark T for true or F for false.

❶ Native Americans did most of the work building
the sawmill. T F

❷ Native Americans were strong and they worked hard. T F

❸ James Marshall told the men to stop working while
he looked at the mill race. T F

❹ Iron pyrite was also called "the blossom of gold." T F

❺ The mill race was connected to the river. T F

C Choose the best answer to each question.

❶ Why do you think people call quartz "the blossom of gold"?

a) because it is so commonly found

b) because it looks like a flower blossom

c) because it is usually found in the same rocks as gold

d) because it is as valuable as gold

❷ What sort of movement did James Brown make with his pan?

a) He tossed it up and down.

b) He moved it from side to side.

c) He swirled it around.

d) He turned it upside down.

D Put the sentences in order according to the sequence of operation of a mill wheel.

❶ The water in the mill race turns the water wheel.

❷ The water from the river rushes along the mill race.

❸ The machinery cuts trees into logs and planks.

❹ The water wheel makes machinery work inside the mill.

_______ → _______ → _______ → _______

Gold Fever

All the men were so excited that they began to dance around, shouting and singing.

"We've found gold!" they cried. "We'll all be rich!"

"Wait," said James Marshall.

"Don't get too excited yet.

We must make sure that there is more gold to be found.

And we must make sure that we stake our claim to it."

"Stake our claim?" called out one man.

"What do you mean?"

"We must make sure that it is only our legal right to dig up this gold," explained James Marshall.

"If we find it, it belongs to us. We don't want other people to come along and take it for their own."

"No, we don't," agreed the men.

James Marshall was a very fair man. He knew that his first job was to finish building Sutter's Mill.

"Stay and help me to finish building the mill," he said.

"Then I will make sure that you get the right to look for more gold here. I will also give you food and tools to do the job."

The men agreed that this sounded fair.

"But there is one thing I want you to promise," said James Marshall.

"This must be kept secret for now. Nobody else must find out about it."

The men agreed once more.

But a few had already crept away while James Marshall was speaking.

They wanted to find their own gold.

They didn't want to share it with everyone else.

Not far from the mill was a small settlement where people lived.

It was called Sutter's Creek.

There was a grocery store in Sutter's Creek.

KEY WORDS

- promise
- keep secret
- for now
- once more
- already
- share
- far

- settlement
- creek
- grocery store
- buy (buy-bought-bought)
- need
- owner
- news

- exciting
- happen
- lately
- feet
- whisper

The men from the mill went there to buy the things that they needed.

The owner was a man called Mr. Smith.

"Hello, boys," he said when some of the men from the mill came in.

"Do you have any news to tell me? Has anything exciting happened to you lately?"

The men looked at each other and they looked at their feet.

They had promised not to say anything about the gold.

But it was just too exciting to keep secret! 

"Gold!" one of them whispered.

"We've found gold out at Sutter's Mill!"

Mr. Smith leaned closer to the men, his eyes gleaming.

"Are you sure?"

The men nodded, and one of them held out his palm.

In it lay one of the gold flakes that James Marshall had discovered.

"This is astonishing news!" gasped Mr. Smith.

"We must let everyone know!"

When the men had gone, Mr. Smith wrote a letter to a newspaper in the nearest town of San Francisco.

The discovery of gold was no longer a secret.

KEY WORDS

- lean
- closer
- palm
- **discover** (*cf.* discovery)
- astonishing
- gasp

- let + A + *Verb*
- **write** (write-wrote-written)
- newspaper
- nearest
- town
- no longer

The men at Sutter's Mill worked hard on the building of the mill.

They had not yet been paid for any of their work.

They wanted to finish it quickly.

But there came a day when the rain was heavy.

It was too wet to work in the mud.

So the men began to search for more gold.

About fifteen miles from the mill, they discovered a rich "prospect".

It was close to a place called Mormon Island. 🌐

KEY WORDS

- wet
- mud
- begin (begin-began-begun)

- search
- mile (= 1609 m)
- prospect

Soon, over a hundred men arrived at Mormon Island.

They wanted to join in the search for gold.

And within weeks, hundreds more came.

They had developed gold fever — not an illness, but the

overwhelming desire to search for gold.

It was more important to them than anything else.

The building of the mill was forgotten.

The men who had arrived to mine for gold were called

"prospectors". Finding the gold was called "prospecting".

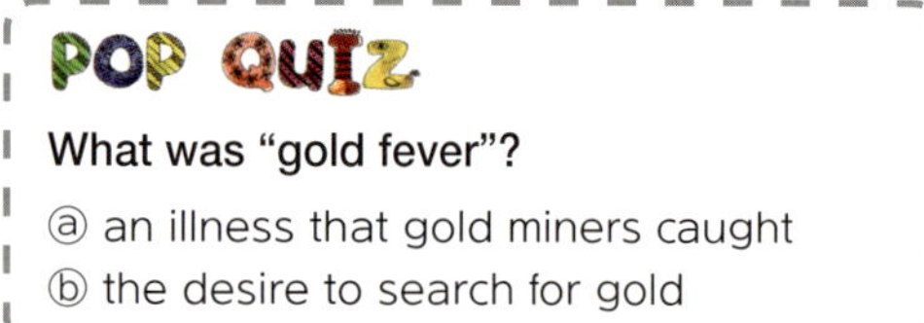

What was "gold fever"?
ⓐ an illness that gold miners caught
ⓑ the desire to search for gold

KEY WORDS

- over
- hundred
- arrive
- join
- within
- develop
- illness
- overwhelming
- desire
- **forget** (forget-forgot-forgotten)
- mine
- prospector
- soil
- remove
- get to
- crack
- realize
- wash
- panning
- in a circular motion
- settle

Soil, sand, and gravel were removed so that the men could get to the rock.

They searched the cracks in the rock for gold.

But then they realized that there might be a better way to find it.

They washed the sand and gravel that they had removed in large pans.

This was called "panning" for gold.

They swirled the pan around in a circular motion and the heavy flakes of gold settled in the bottom. (Aha!)

But it was difficult, slow work.

▲ gold panning

Then, a man called Alexander Stephens had an idea.

He made a wooden trough.

He left the bottom round so that it rocked from side to side.

This became known as a gold rocker. Aha!

Into the rocker he put sand and gravel that had been scraped off the rocks.

Water ran into the rocker, and Alexander Stephens rocked it from side to side.

The gold settled on the bottom of the rocker.

▲ collecting gold using a rocker

When the rocker was put on a slope, the gold slid to the bottom. From there, it was easy to collect.

When enough gold had collected, it was tipped into a tub of clean water.

At the end of each day, the gold was cleaned and weighed.

It was weighed on a pair of wooden scales.

Silver coins were used as weights to balance the scales.

One silver dollar weighed the same as one ounce of gold.

What were used as weights to balance the scales?
ⓐ gold coins
ⓑ silver coins

KEY WORDS

- **trough**
- **from side to side** (*cf.* side)
- **become known** (become-became-become)
- **rocker**
- **scrape off**
- **run** (run-ran-run)
- **slope**
- **slide** (slide-slid-slid)
- **collect**
- **enough**
- **tip**
- **tub**
- **clean**
- **weigh**
- **a pair of scales** (*cf.* scale)
- **silver**
- **coin**
- **weight**
- **balance**
- **ounce** (= 28.35 g)

While the miners at Mormon Island were prospecting for more gold, the news was spreading.

In May, 1848, a man ran around San Francisco with a bottle filled with gold dust.

He came from Sutter's Creek. "Gold! Gold from American River!" he shouted.

That was the first proof that there really was gold.

It was then that the rush to the gold fields began.

- miner
- **spread** (spread-spread-spread)
- bottle
- dust
- proof
- gold field
- harbor
- **bring** (bring-brought-brought)

- seek one's[a] fortune
  (seek-sought-sought)(*cf.* fortune)
- coast
- village
- empty
- leave behind
- learn
- skill

- take on
- task
- care for
- alone
- farm
- even
- outside

San Francisco harbor soon filled with boats.

The boats brought men to seek their fortune.

All along the coast, towns and villages emptied of men.

They left their jobs and hurried to the gold fields.

The women were left behind. They had to learn new skills and take on new tasks.

They cared for their families alone and kept the businesses running.

They farmed the land and worked even harder than they had before.

And then the news spread even further… outside California.

▲ the San Francisco harbor around 1850

(See page for author [Public domain], via Wikimedia Commons)

Comprehension Quiz

A Fill in each blank with the right word below to complete each sentence.

small	exciting	fair	secret

❶ The men thought that James Marshall's offer sounded

_______________.

❷ The men agreed that the discovery of gold must be kept

_______________.

❸ Sutter's Creek was a _______________ settlement where people lived.

❹ The grocery store owner asked if anything _______________ had happened lately.

B Put the sentences in order according to the process of extracting gold.

❶ The men swirled the pan around in a circular motion.

❷ The men added water to the pan.

❸ Heavy gold particles settled at the bottom of the pan.

❹ The men dug up sand and gravel from the bottom of the river.

_______ → _______ → _______ → _______

C Choose the best answer to each question.

❶ What was a gold rocker made of?

a) rock　　　　　　　　b) gold

c) wood　　　　　　　　d) silver

❷ Why did most of the men leave the towns and villages along the coast?

a) They wanted to give the women a chance to be farmers.

b) They moved to San Francisco to open businesses.

c) They sailed away to other countries.

d) They went to search for gold and make their fortune.

D Circle the person who said each line.

❶ "Hello, boys. Do you have any news to tell me?" **Mr. Smith / James Marshall**

❷ "Nobody else must find out about it." **Mr. Smith / James Marshall**

❸ "We must let everyone know!" **Mr. Smith / James Marshall**

❹ "We must make sure that we stake our claim to it." **Mr. Smith / James Marshall**

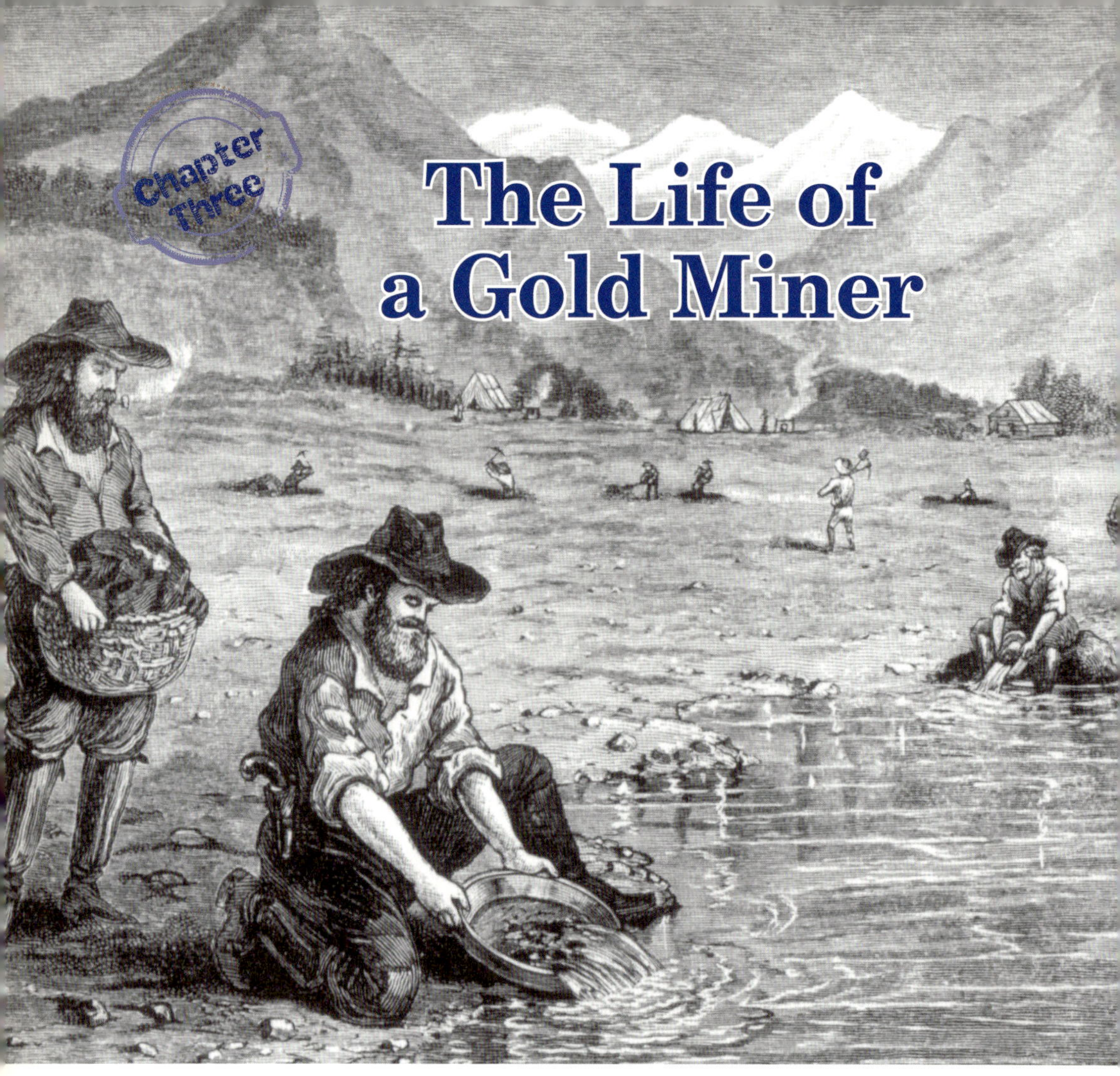

The Life of a Gold Miner

The news of the gold discovery next reached the state of Oregon.

"You can go to California and find gold!" the people told each other.

They talked about it in the streets and in their homes.

They talked about it wherever they went.

They could hardly believe it!

"Wherever you find gold, you can stake a claim and keep prospecting there," one of them said.

"It doesn't cost anything to start prospecting.

All you need are simple tools and some water.

All the gold that you find belongs to you!

You can sell it and become rich."

Men set off in horse-drawn wagons.

They left behind their wives, their children, and their homes.

Canada
China & Other Countries
the United States
San Francisco
Gold Fields
Hawaii
Mexico
Pacific Ocean
Central America

Soon after them came men from Hawaii.

They crossed the sea in boats through rough weather.

More men came from Mexico and Central America.

Soon, Mormon Island became overcrowded with people.

By the end of the year, it seemed that the whole world had heard the news.

Even as far away as China, people heard that there was gold in the United States.

Even more men came.

▲ Chinese gold miners
(By Photographer: Graves, Roy D. (Roy Daniel), 1889-1971
(Chinese, Gold Mining in California) [Public domain], via Wikimedia Commons)

KEY WORDS

- cross
- rough
- weather

- Mexico
- Central America
- overcrowded

- as A as B
- China

▲ geographical factors that made the trip to California difficult
(The left side is the Sierra Nevada mountain range and the right side is Death Valley.)

By 1849, there were men from many different countries.

The men who rushed to California in 1849 were called the "forty-niners".

They all came because they wanted to be rich.

They were all overcome with gold fever!

But the journey was long, difficult, and very dangerous.

Many of the men who traveled to California walked there.

They came all the way from Canada or the eastern United States.

For many, it was a journey of more than 2,000 km.

It took up to nine months.

They faced terrible winter weather.

Many of them suffered from frostbite or froze to death.

Others died of starvation because they didn't have enough food with them on the journey.

Some died of diseases such as cholera.

Others simply gave up, exhausted and unable to go any further.

What were the men who came to the gold fields in 1849 called?

ⓐ forty-niners
ⓑ gold rockers

KEY WORDS

- country
- overcome (overcome-overcame-overcome)
- journey
- dangerous
- travel
- all the way from
- eastern
- up to
- terrible
- suffer from
- frostbite
- freeze to death (freeze-froze-frozen)
- die of
- starvation
- disease
- such as
- cholera
- simply
- give up (give-gave-given)
- exhausted
- unable to + *Verb* (↔ able)

▲ the advertisement of a liner that sailed from the eastern states of the USA to San Francisco
(By - G.F. Nesbitt & Co., printer [Public domain], via Wikimedia Commons)

Some men sold everything they owned.

They paid for a ticket on a ship to San Francisco.

Some had to sail from one side of America right round to the other.

Others endured the long sea voyage from China, Germany, Ireland, Turkey, and France.

When they arrived in California, they found that thousands of men were already there.

They had already found a lot of gold.

The new men wondered if there was any left for them.

What if it had all gone? 

But they didn't give up.

They got to work and began prospecting for gold.

Some people improved the gold rocker.

They invented the sluice box.

A sluice box was a long wooden trough around 30 cm wide.

It had a metal sheet in the bottom of it.

▲ a sluice box used in modern times

POP QUIZ

What was invented by the prospectors?
ⓐ gold
ⓑ sluice box

KEY WORDS

- ticket
- ship
- sail
- endure
- voyage
- Germany

- Ireland
- Turkey
- France
- thousands of
- wonder
- all gone

- get to work
- improve
- invent
- sluice
- wide
- metal sheet

The metal sheet had small holes in it.

Underneath the holes was a riffle box.

This was a box with small ledges, or "riffles" built into it.

Water rushed through the box.

The heavy gold and some sand fell through the holes.

The gold fell into the riffle box and caught on the riffles.

Twice a day, miners removed the gold and sand from the riffles.

KEY WORDS

- underneath
- riffle
- ledge

- built into
- **catch** (catch-caught-caught)
- twice

Then they panned what was on the riffles.

This separated the gold from the sand.

Mercury was also added to the sluice boxes.

It attached itself to the gold.

This made the gold heavier, so that it fell through the holes more easily. But this was dangerous. The miners didn't know that mercury was very poisonous.

▲ mercury

KEY WORDS

- separate
- mercury
- add
- attach oneself to
- poisonous

The miners worked hard and some of them found plenty of gold.

Their dreams came true.

But for most of the miners, life was difficult.

The land was extremely crowded.

In 1848, there were around 800 white people in California.

There were also many Native Americans. They were the original inhabitants of the land.

The white people had come later.

KEY WORDS

- plenty of
- dream
- come true
- extremely
- original

- inhabitant
- argument
- break out
- fighting (*cf.* fight(fight-fought-fought))
- stealing (*cf.* steal)

- cheating (*cf.* cheat)
- lying (*cf.* lie)
- gambling (*cf.* gamble)
- win (win-won-won)
- gamble away

By the end of 1849, there were around 100,000 new people!

They were all searching for gold.

Many arguments broke out.

A lot of fighting, stealing, cheating, and lying went on.

Gambling was a big problem.

Some men won thousands of dollars in one night.

But often, they gambled it all away again. Then, they had nothing left at all.

Men from one country fought against those of another country.

Thieves tried to steal the gold that belonged to Chinese people.

But the Chinese people were very clever.

They melted their gold and made pots and cups out of it.

They covered the golden pots in black dirt to make them look worthless.

Nobody took any notice of the laws.

There weren't enough lawmen to watch everyone.

It was a very harsh life.

Why did the Chinese people melt their gold?
ⓐ to hide their pots
ⓑ to hide their gold

KEY WORDS

- **thief** (*cf.* thieves)
- Chinese
- clever
- melt
- pot

- out of
- cover
- dirt
- worthless
- take notice of

- law
- lawman
- watch
- harsh

To begin with, miners lived in camps that were made up of tents and cabins. Six or seven miners lived in each cabin.

▲ a cabin where gold miners lived

The cabin had windows, a fireplace, and an oven for cooking.

But there were no toilets or comfortable chairs.

Food was plain, and there wasn't enough of it.

Many miners fell ill.

The ones who didn't fall ill were often lonely.

They wanted to go home.

But many of them never went home again.

POP QUIZ

What was not in the miners' cabin?
ⓐ toilet
ⓑ fireplace

KEY WORDS

- to begin with
- be made up of
- fireplace

- toilet
- comfortable
- plain

- fall ill
- lonely
- never

Where people settled, mining towns grew up.

Some people opened shops to serve the miners.

Other businesses grew up, too.

After all, the miners needed food, houses, and mining equipment.

They needed horses, mules, and wagons to transport their goods.

The miners also needed banks to take care of their gold and their money.

▲ a mining town in 1849

KEY WORDS

- **grow up** (grow-grew-grown)
- **shop** (= store)
- **serve**
- **equipment**
- **mule**
- **transport**
- **goods**
- **take care of**

▲ Levi Strauss
(See page for author [Public domain],
via Wikimedia Commons)

In 1853, one man called Levi Strauss had a good idea. He saw that miners needed strong clothing that would not tear easily.
He took some brown tent canvas that was very strong.
He made it into trousers.
The miners wore the trousers when they worked.
The trousers were very popular.
They were also cheap, and comfortable to wear.
After a while, Levi Strauss began to use denim instead of canvas.

KEY WORDS

- clothing
- tear (tear-tore-torn)
- canvas
- trousers
- popular
- cheap
- after a while
- denim
- instead of

Denim was a strong fabric,
originally made in
France.
Levi Strauss dyed it
dark blue.
And this is how blue
jeans began!

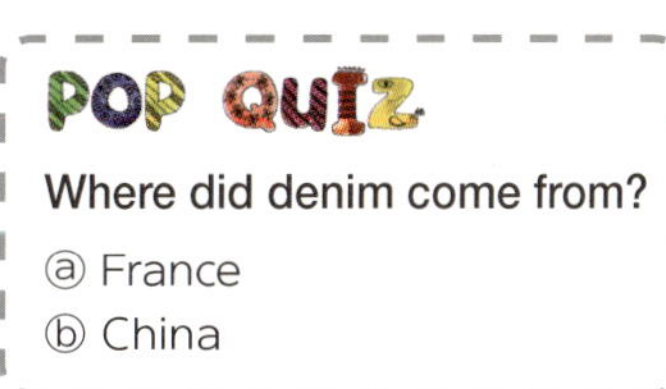

Millions of people around the world still wear them today.

Many men who were poor at finding gold made their

fortune in business instead.

Saloons (public drinking houses) were very popular.

But people often did more gambling than drinking in such

places.

Women came to live in the towns with the men.

Their lives were just as difficult and dangerous.

KEY WORDS

- fabric
- dye
- dark
- blue jeans
- millions of
- be poor at
- make one's fortune
- saloon
- public
- such

Chapter Three

Comprehension Quiz

A Fill in each blank with the right word below to complete each sentence.

through	behind	to	on

❶ The men left _______________ their wives, their children, and their homes.

❷ The men crossed the sea in boats _______________ rough weather.

❸ The gold fell into the riffle box and got caught _______________ the riffles.

❹ The journey to California took up _______________ nine months.

B Circle the right word for each underlined part.

❶ The land was (extremely / extremly) crowded.

❷ Many (arguements / arguments) broke out.

❸ Men from one country (fought / fourght) against those from another country.

❹ After all, the miners needed food, houses, and mining (equeepment / equipment).

C Choose the best answer to each question.

❶ Who originally lived in California?

a) Chinese people   b) Hawaiian people

c) Canadian people   d) Native Americans

❷ How did the miners transport their goods?

a) They used river boats.

b) They used horses, mules, and wagons.

c) They used handcars on railroad tracks.

d) They used tractors.

D Find and underline the words that need to change places in the sentence as the following example shows.

Denim was a strong <u>France</u>, originally made in <u>fabric</u>.

❶ They covered the black pots in golden dirt to make them look worthless.

❷ Nobody took any laws of the notice.

❸ Some men won dollars of thousands in one night.

❹ Some people opened miners to serve the shops.

Chapter Four

King Midas and the Golden Touch

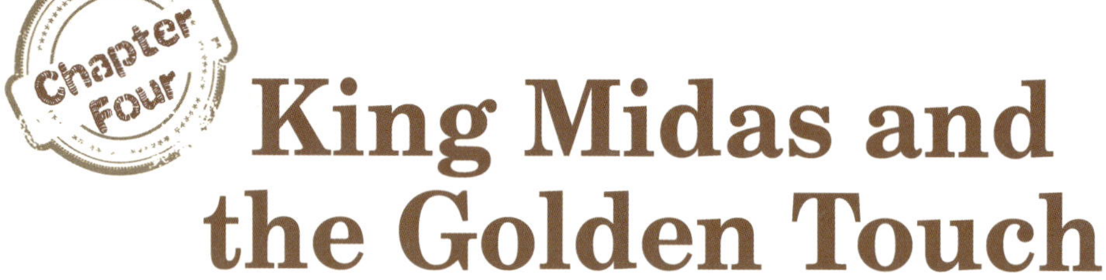

In the evenings, the miners were tired from working all day.

They missed their homes.

Some of them sang songs or told stories.

"Why do so many people love gold?" asked a young miner one night.

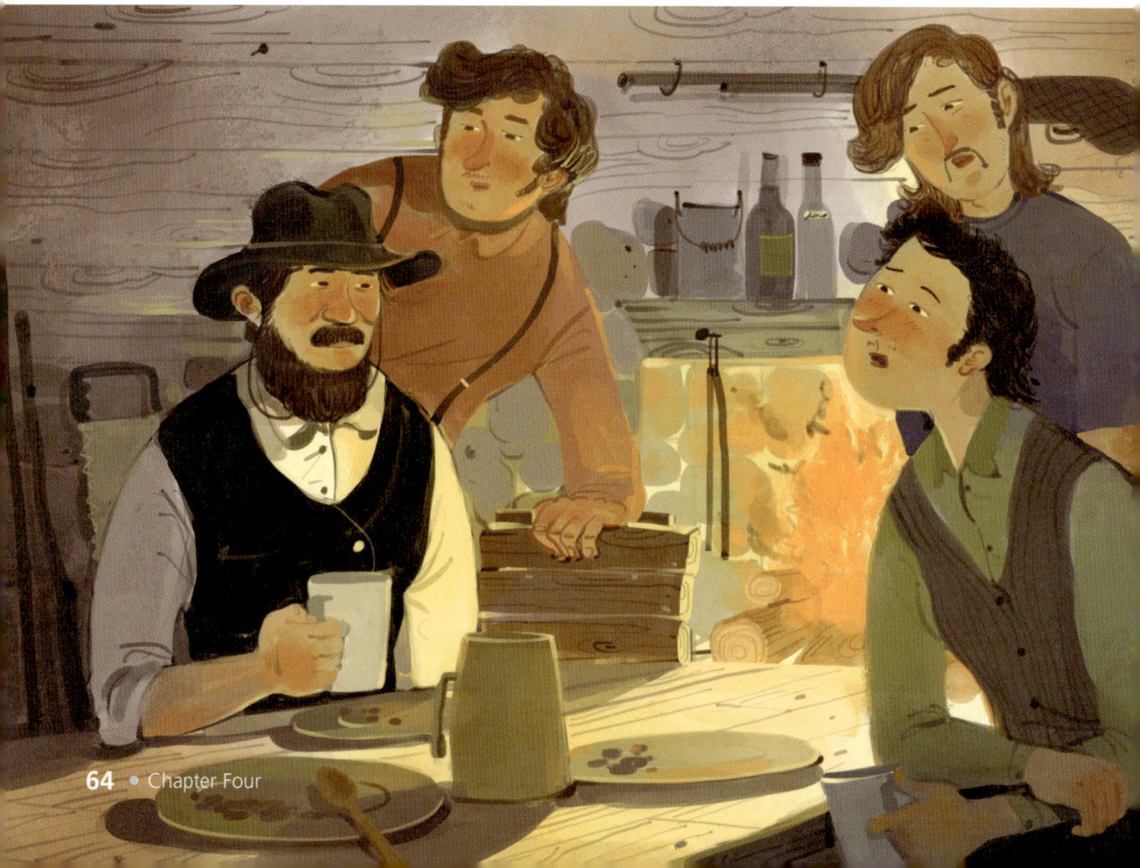

"We have all given up everything, just to have gold."

Another miner, who was older and wiser, answered him.

"We're not the first people to have gold fever," he said. 

"We're not?" The young miner looked surprised.

"No. Thousands of years ago, in ancient Greece, there was a king called Midas. He wanted gold even more than we do. But it almost destroyed his life."

The other miners gathered around. They begged the old miner to tell them the story.

"Very well," said the old miner.

This is the story that he told:

KEY WORDS

- touch
- miss
- wise

- surprised
- ancient
- almost

- destroy
- beg
- Very well.

The Story of King Midas

Midas was a great king, who ruled a great kingdom.

He had everything he needed.

In fact, he had more than that — he had everything he wished for.

Midas lived in a beautiful palace surrounded by amazing gardens. They were full of flowers and trees.

Their scent was like perfume.

He loved to walk in the garden and enjoy everything that he
owned.

He liked to spend his days counting all his money and
looking at his stores of gold.

"Ah, it is gold that has brought me such blessing!" he thought.

One day, Midas was walking in his garden when he came
across a satyr — a man with a horse's ears and a horse's tail.

The satyr's name was Silenus. He was a friend of Dionysus,
the god of wine and pleasure.

He was lost, and had wandered into the king's garden.

KEY WORDS

- great
- rule
- kingdom
- in fact
- wish for
- palace
- surrounded by
- amazing
- be full of
- scent
- perfume
- spend
- count
- store
- blessing
- one day
- come across
- satyr
- wine
- pleasure
- lost
- wander

Midas was delighted to find such an important guest in his garden, so he invited Silenus to stay.

For ten days, Midas gave feasts for his guest.

In return, Silenus entertained Midas and his friends with songs and stories.

When the ten days were over, Midas left the palace and took Silenus back to Dionysus.

The god was pleased to see Silenus.

He said, "Midas, I wish to show you my thanks for bringing my friend back to me.

I will give you whatever you wish for."

Midas thought for a while. "Don't I have everything I need?" he asked himself. 
But then his greedy thoughts turned toward gold.

"What if I could have more gold? What if everything I touched would turn into gold?" he wondered.

"I wish that everything I touch will turn into gold," he said. "Give me the golden touch."

"Your wish will come true," said Dionysus.

KEY WORDS

- **for a while** (= for a moment)
- **ask oneself**
- **greedy**
- **thought**
- **turn toward**
- **turn into[to]**

Midas went home to his palace.

As he walked through the gardens, Midas admired the beautiful roses that grew there.

He reached out to touch one.

Instantly, it turned to gold in his hand!

He stroked the smooth, hard petals and touched the other roses nearby.

Soon all the bushes were covered with gold roses!

They no longer had a beautiful scent, but Midas didn't care.

"I really do have the golden touch!" he laughed.

KEY WORDS

- admire
- reach out
- instantly
- stroke
- smooth
- petal
- bush
- be covered with
- care
- laugh

Midas wanted to celebrate his good fortune.

He ordered his servants to prepare a huge feast.

They brought all kinds of good food — olives and grapes,

roasted meat and jugs of wine.

Midas was very hungry after his walk.

He reached for a bunch of juicy grapes.

But before he could put one into his mouth, the bunch turned hard and cold.

All the grapes had turned into glittering gold!

KEY WORDS

- celebrate
- order
- servant
- prepare
- all kinds of
- olive
- a bunch of
- grape(s)
- roasted
- jug
- juicy
- glittering

At first, Midas smiled and laughed.

Now he would be the richest man in the whole world!

But when he tried to pour some wine, the wine turned solid in the jug.

When he reached for a slice of roasted meat, it turned as hard as a rock.

Midas's face turned pale with fright.

His stomach rumbled with hunger.

"What shall I do?" he cried.

"If I cannot eat, then I will starve to death!"

KEY WORDS

- richest
- pour
- solid
- a slice of
- pale
- fright
- stomach
- rumble
- hunger
- starve to death

At that moment, Midas's daughter came in to share the meal.

When she saw Midas's pale face, she hurried to his side.

"What is wrong, Father?" she asked.

Midas threw his arms around his daughter. He held her close,

needing the comfort of a warm hug.

But he found himself holding a cold, hard statue made of gold.

"What have I done?" cried Midas.

"My greed has destroyed all the good things in my life."

He was sorry that he had ever been so greedy.

He wished that he had never asked for the golden touch.

Midas fell to his knees and prayed to Dionysus to help him.

Dionysus appeared to Midas and gave him some instructions:

"You must go to the river called Pactolus," said Dionysus. 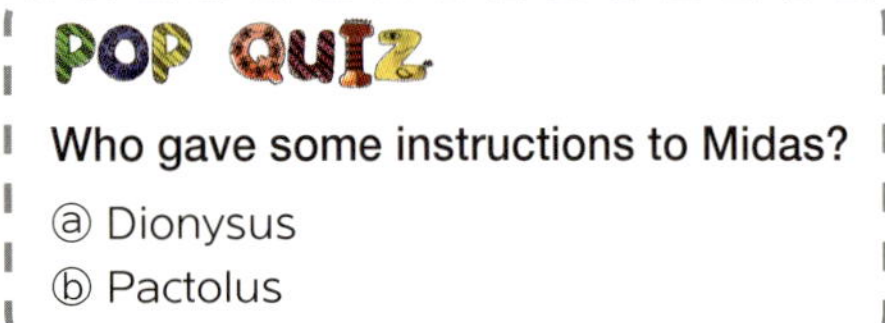

"There you must wash in the waters.

All your power will flow into the river instead."

So Midas hurried to the river.

On the way, he was careful not to touch anything or anyone.

POP QUIZ

Who gave some instructions to Midas?
ⓐ Dionysus
ⓑ Pactolus

KEY WORDS

- sorry
- fall to one's knees
- pray
- appear (↔ disappear)
- instruction
- power
- on the way
- careful
- as + *Adverb* + as + *Subject* + can
- afraid

He knelt by the river and put his hands deep into the flowing water.

All his power flowed into the river.

Little flakes of gold fell into the water.

"Has the golden touch really left me?" wondered Midas.

He rushed home as quickly as he could.

He was afraid that his daughter was still a statue.

But as he approached the castle, she came running out to
meet him.

She was soft and warm, and she was full of joy at seeing him.

The wonderful scent of roses filled the garden once more.

Midas vowed that he would never be so greedy again.

But ever since then, the waters of the river
Pactolus have been rich with gold.

The old miner finished his story.

The other miners sat silently for a moment.

They wondered whether their own greed for gold was destroying their lives, just like Midas.

"Is that why our river is filled with gold?" the youngest miner asked.

The old miner smiled and shook his head.

"It's just a story," he said.

POP QUIZ

How did Midas know that his golden touch really left him?

ⓐ His castle was filled with scent again.
ⓑ His castle was filled with gold again.

KEY WORDS

- approach
- castle
- joy
- wonderful

- vow
- ever since then
- sit (sit-sat-sat)
- silently

- whether
- youngest

"Our river is filled with small pieces of gold that have washed loose from the rocks.

The rocks have been there for thousands of years.

The river erodes them." 

"Erodes them?" the youngest one asked.

"What does that mean?"

"It means that the river wears the rock away.

Some of the gold breaks off.

It washes into the water so that we can find it."

KEY WORDS

- loose
- erode
- wear away
- break off
- thriving
- visit
- tourist

▲ Golden Gate Bridge, the symbol of San Francisco

After several years of mining, it became more and more difficult to find gold.

People turned to other ways of making money.

The mining towns became better places to live in.

San Francisco became a large and thriving city.

People from many different countries lived there.

Even today, many people live there and many others visit as tourists every year.

People still go to California to seek their fortune.

But they are no longer mining for gold.

Some want to become famous movie stars.

Others hope to become rich in the technology industry.

Others just hope for a better life in the golden sunshine.

But some bad memories remain.

During the Gold Rush, many Native Americans were attacked.

They were forced off their land.

They were pushed out of their own homes and left with nowhere to go.

And there is still some mercury in the soil in some places.

It poisons the soil and the fish in some of the rivers.

So was the California Gold Rush a good thing, or a bad thing?

Some people became very rich and made their fortunes.

Other people lost everything, including their homes or their lives.

Good or bad, the Gold Rush changed the lives of thousands of people forever.

POP QUIZ

Who were forced off their land during the Gold Rush?
ⓐ the forty-niners
ⓑ Native Americans

KEY WORDS

- technology
- industry
- sunshine
- memory
- remain

- during
- attack
- force off
- push
- poison

- lose (lose-lost-lost)
- including
- change
- forever

Comprehension Quiz

A Who is the subject 'I' in the following sentence? Choose and circle.

❶ I enjoyed the feasts that the king gave for me.

Midas / Dionysus / Silenus

❷ I was glad to see my friend return from the palace.

Midas / Dionysus / Silenus

❸ I told stories and sang songs to the king and his friends.

Midas / Dionysus / Silenus

❹ I was delighted to find a satyr in my garden.

Midas / Dionysus / Silenus

B Fill in each blank with the right word below to complete each sentence.

admired	turned	wondered	wandered

❶ He was lost, and had _____________ into the king's garden.

❷ As he walked through the gardens, Midas _____________ the beautiful roses that grew there.

❸ When he tried to pour some wine, the wine _____________ solid in the jug.

❹ They _____________ whether their own greed for gold was destroying their lives, just like Midas.

 Choose the best answer to each question.

❶ How did Dionysus show his thanks to King Midas?

a) Dionysus said that he would give King Midas whatever he wished for.

b) Dionysus shook King Midas's hand.

c) Dionysus said that he would give King Midas a daughter.

d) Dionysus said that Silenus could stay at the palace forever.

❷ What were King Midas's emotions when he realized that his wish had come true?

a) First, he was afraid. Then, he was happy.

b) First, he was angry. Then, he was afraid.

c) First, he was happy. Then, he was afraid.

d) First, he was sad. Then, he was angry.

D Mark T for true or F for false.

❶ The young miner was wiser than the old miner. T F

❷ The Californian miners were the first people to have gold fever. T F

❸ Many gold miners gave up everything, just to find gold. T F

❹ King Midas lived thousands of years before the Californian miners. T F

Let's Review the Story

Fill in the blanks to review the story.

Title: ______________ !

Chapter 1: ______________

- James M______ saw a white rock in the r______.
- James B______ t______ it to see what it was.
- They found that they had discovered g______.

Chapter 2: ______________

- Some men told the s______ about the d______ of g______.
- Alexander Stephens invented the g______ r______ so that they could get more gold.
- Lots more people came to C______ to look for g______.

Chapter 3: The Life of a Gold Miner

- Men made difficult, dangerous j______s to reach C______.
- Life in a m______ settlement was h______. A lot of f______, st______, c______, and lying went on.
- Lots of new b______ grew up and the mining settlements grew into town.

Chapter 4: King Midas and the Golden Touch

- The m______ told each other st______. One was called " T______ S______ of K______ M______ ".
- King Midas was gr______ for g______, but it almost d______ his life. After that, he was s______ and he ch______ his ways.
- The California G______ R______ was g______ for some people and b______ for others.

Let's Think & Talk

Think about the following questions and answer them freely.

❶ Imagine that you are living in 1848 and you hear the news about the California Gold Rush one day. You could be rich if you found gold, but it is also possible that you wouldn't be able to find gold at all. Would you leave your home and join the California Gold Rush? Tell us your choice and the reason.

❷ Research what kind of living environment immigrants during the gold rush period lived in. Now imagine you are living in a town created by the California Gold Rush. What would be the hardest aspect of daily life?

❸ What influence did the California Gold Rush have on the different regions of California? Find examples of good and bad influences and tell us about them.

❹ If you could, would you want to have King Midas's golden touch? Also tell us the reason why you think that way.

Let's Review the Story

Title: Gold Rush !

Chapter 1: Discovery

- James Marshall saw a white rock in the river.
- James Brown tested it to see what it was.
- They found that they had discovered gold.

Chapter 2: Gold Fever

- Some men told the secret about the discovery of gold.
- Alexander Stephens invented the gold rocker so that they could get more gold.
- Lots more people came to California to look for gold.

Chapter 3: The Life of a Gold Miner

- Men made difficult, dangerous journeys to reach California.
- Life in a mining settlement was harsh. A lot of fighting, stealing, cheating, and lying went on.
- Lots of new businesses grew up and the mining settlements grew into town.

Chapter 4: King Midas and the Golden Touch

- The miners told each other stories. One was called " The Story of King Midas ".
- King Midas was greedy for gold, but it almost destroyed his life. After that, he was sorry and he changed his ways.
- The California Gold Rush was good for some people and bad for others.

- Gold Rush!
- Level 4
- 25 Questions

(Vocabulary 5 / Reading Comprehension 16 /

Sentence Structure & Grammar 4)

※ Choose the word which has the similar meaning. (1~2)

1. improve
   ① dislike
   ② make better
   ③ steal
   ④ take apart

2. popular
   ① strong
   ② comfortable
   ③ difficult to make
   ④ liked by many people

3. What is a "mill race"?
   ① a type of tree used for making wooden planks
   ② a contest to see who can dig the fastest
   ③ a narrow channel of fast moving water
   ④ a machine inside a mill that cuts pieces of wood

4. In the following sentence, what does it mean to "stake a claim"?

> Wherever you find gold, you can <u>stake a claim</u> and keep prospecting there.

   ① to make sure that everyone knows that gold has been found
   ② to make sure that only the person who found the gold can dig it up
   ③ to make sure that anyone can come and take the gold from that place
   ④ to make sure that nobody knows that gold was found in a certain place

5. What is the common word for the two blanks?

> • His voice was filled _____________ disappointment.
> • All the bushes were covered _____________ gold roses!

① on   ② by
③ for   ④ with

6. What did James Marshall see in the river first?
   ① fish   ② gold
   ③ coins   ④ quartz

7. Why did James Brown bite a gold flake?
   ① He wanted to see if it tasted of anything.
   ② He wanted to see if it would break his teeth.
   ③ He wanted to see if his teeth would leave bite marks.
   ④ He wanted to see if he could bite straight through it.

8. How did James Brown know that he had found gold, and not fool's gold?
   ① When he hit it with a hammer, it broke into pieces.
   ② When he hit it with a hammer, it did not break into pieces.
   ③ When he hit it with a hammer, the hammer broke into pieces.
   ④ When he hit it with a hammer, the hammer left marks on it.

9. What is a "prospect"?
   ① a type of shop
   ② an island in the middle of a river
   ③ a Native American settlement
   ④ an area of land on which gold has been discovered

10. Which of these did men NOT use to reach the gold fields?

   ① boats

   ② airplanes

   ③ their own feet

   ④ horse-drawn wagons

11. Why were some of the men disappointed when they arrived in California?

   ① A lot of gold had already been found.

   ② There was no more gold left to be found.

   ③ They faced terrible winter weather.

   ④ There was nowhere for them to live.

12. Why is mercury dangerous?

   ① It is very heavy.

   ② It destroys gold.

   ③ It is poisonous.

   ④ It can't be seen easily.

13. How did the Chinese people hide their gold?

   ① They buried it in the ground.

   ② They sent it back to China on a boat.

   ③ They covered it with dirt.

   ④ They hid it in their cabins.

14. What was Levi Strauss's "good idea"?

   ① He opened a bank for the miners.

   ② He sold mules to the miners.

   ③ He ran a saloon for the miners.

   ④ He made trousers for the miners.

15. What sort of clothing did the miners need?
　① clothing that was brown
　② clothing that was easy to wash
　③ clothing that was strong
　④ clothing that was cool

16. Which of these things did King Midas like to do best? Choose *two* answers.
　① He liked to walk in his garden.
　② He liked to visit the river.
　③ He liked to count his money.
　④ He liked to sing and dance.

17. What is a "satyr"?
　① a horse with a man's ears
　② a man with a horse's eyes
　③ a horse with a man's legs
　④ a man with a horse's ears and tail

18. Why did the roses lose their scent in Midas's gardens?
　① They grew old and dried up.
　② They turned into solid gold.
　③ They were picked and put into vases.
　④ They were eaten by bugs.

19. Why was King Midas upset when he hugged his daughter?
　① She did not want him to hug her.
　② She turned into gold.
　③ She made him hug a statue instead.
　④ She told him to go away.

20. What did Dionysus tell King Midas to do?
    ① to walk in his garden
    ② to give away all of his gold
    ③ to wash himself in the river
    ④ to wash his daughter in the river

21. Why was the Gold Rush a bad thing for the Native Americans?
    ① They all got poisoned by the mercury.
    ② They gambled away all of their gold.
    ③ They were forced off their land and they lost their homes.
    ④ They became greedy and fought each other.

22. What is the wrong part of the sentence?

Are that why our river is filled with gold?
① ② ③ ④

※ Choose the correct sentence. (23~24)
23. ① But it was just too exciting to keep secret!
    ② But it was just so exciting that to keep secret!
    ③ But it was just to excting too keep secret!
    ④ But it was too exciting so to keep secret!

24. ① Then they panned that was on the riffles.

② Then they panned it was on the riffles.

③ Then they panned what was on the riffles.

④ Then they panned which was on the riffles.

25. What is the proper word for the blank?

> It was then _____________ the rush to the gold fields began.

① at

② that

③ this

④ to

Sarah J. Dodd

Sarah J. Dodd is an experienced primary school teacher who resides in the UK, but has also lived and taught in Australia. She has a PhD in Science and a certificate in Creative Writing. She has published several books for children: "An Angel Anyway" (Anyway Press, 2008) the "Little Angels" series (Lion Children's Books, 2009/10), "The Lion Picture Bible" (Lion Children's Books, 2015) and "Legs: the tale of a meerkat lost and found" (Lion Children's Books, 2015). Her poetry for children has also been highly commended and published in the anthology "Let in the Stars" (Manchester Metropolitan University, 2014).
She is currently working on further picture books for the very young, and a novel for older children.

Gold Rush!

Written by Sarah J. Dodd
Illustrated by Juyeon Kim

First Published in August 2016

Editorial Manager: Juyon Choi
Editors: Juyon Choi, Myungjin Kim, Kyunghee Jang, Jiyeong Park
Designers: Eunhee Lee, Elim
Cover Designer: Eunhee Lee

Published and distributed by

Darakwon Bldg., 64-1 Jandari-ro, Mapo-gu, Seoul, Korea 04031
Tel: 82-2-736-2031(ext. 250)   Fax: 82-2-732-2037
Homepage: www.ihappyhouse.co.kr
Publisher: Kyudo Chung

ISBN: 978-89-6653-411-1 18740 / 978-89-6653-156-1 18740(set)

[Components]
• 1 Audio CD (Recording Studio: Aram)
• Answer Keys & Korean Translation: Free download at www.ihappyhouse.co.kr